SIMPLY
CURTAINS
50 CREATIVE IDEAS FOR DRAPES, BLINDS,& VALANCES

LINDA BARKER
PHOTOGRAPHY BY LIZZIE ORME

SIMPLY

CURTAINS

50 CREATIVE IDEAS FOR DRAPES, BLINDS, & VALANCES

LINDA BARKER
PHOTOGRAPHY BY LIZZIE ORME

CRESCENT
BOOKS
New York · Avenel

For Alexander, Sara, Sarah and Andrew

This 1996 edition is published by Crescent Books,
a division of Random House Value Publishing, Inc.,
40 Engelhard Avenue, Avenel, New Jersey 07001.

Crescent Books and colophon are trademarks of
Random House Value Publishing, Inc.

Random House
New York ● Toronto ● London ● Sydney ● Auckland

Copyright © Collins & Brown Ltd 1995

Editor	Emma Callery
Assistant Project Designer	Petra Boase
Design	Watermark Communications Group Ltd
Photographer	Lizzie Orme
Assisted by	Sussie Bell
Stylist	Linda Barker
Jacket Design	Watermark Communications Group Ltd

A CIP catalog record for this book is available
from the Library of Congress.

ISBN 0–517–15988–0
Typeset in Great Britain by
Watermark Communications Group Ltd
Color reproduction by Daylight, Singapore

Printed and bound by Graficromo s.a., Cordoba, Spain

8 7 6 5 4 3 2 1

Contents

Introduction
6

INTRODUCTION

All homes have windows that need covering. Whether your home really is a castle or just one room, it doesn't matter. Windows are all made of glass, and coverings are designed either to stop people looking in at you, or to prevent you from looking out at them, or onto a brick wall or an ugly power station. Coverings may be designed to keep heat in or keep it out, or they are simply positioned around, above or in front of a window as a form of decoration. There are lots of reasons why we have the coverings we have. More often than not, they are there because that was all that was available at the time, or the first expense in a new home meant that we had to compromise. Whatever the reason, we all have windows to cover and there are lots of people working as professional designers that will tell you that you'll need lined, interlined, swagged, goblet-pleated extravagant window coverings that may look fabulous but will undoubtably cost the earth. But I'll let you in on a secret - you don't have to have the advice of an expert or the bank account of an oil magnate. Windows can be chic and cheap. Not only are the materials inexpensive to buy but the results can look stunning and there's something here to please most tastes.

In SIMPLY CURTAINS I'll show you how to cover all sorts of windows - for baby's rooms, living rooms, kitchens or bathrooms. I'll give you inspiring ideas for transforming your existing curtains or ideas for a complete overhaul. Pelmets, tiebacks, holdbacks and window boxes are all outlined in this book, along with detailed step-by-step photographs. I hope not only to inspire you with fifty project ideas, but to make their construction easier than you think.

It is surprising how few materials you need to transform your existing

curtains yet still manage to completely rejuvenate them. A twisted corded heading is about the simplest thing you could do to a pair of curtains and only involves hand stitching a simple cord around the gathered heading. Of course, you needn't spend any money at all: the plaited knits tieback will soon take care of those shrunken woollens that you have been meaning to take to the charity shop. Shrink them even further through the hottest wash programme in your washing machine and cut the shrunken felted results into long thin strips, plait them together and sew! That's all there is to it; soft felted tiebacks for the price of, well, a hot wash!

I love the idea of constructing something useful from odd pieces and scraps of fabric. I'm sure we could all have a desirable house if we had plenty of money to lavish on the decoration but let's face it, not many people have the spending power of a bored housewife in St Tropez or Palm Beach. And, to tell the truth, it is very rewarding and satisfying to sit back and think, "I did that! and I didn't have to spend a fortune!"

I also love the idea of decorating a child's room with simple decorations that you would not find in any designer showroom or department store. The soft padded numbers, for example, are quickly stitched, and they have pull-off touch-and-close fastener sewn to the underside and its opposite strip is sewn directly onto the curtain. In this way the numbers hang decoratively from the curtain but can be easily removed and replaced as an educational toy.

I've always enjoyed working with ideas that are amusing and stimulating as well as decorative and practical and I hope you enjoy my ideas in this, the sixth book of the series, SIMPLY CURTAINS.

Getting Started

It is vital to take accurate measurements when you are considering making any type of window decoration. A little time spent with your retractible tape measure at the beginning of your project is time well spent. Jot the measurements onto a notebook so that they are at hand throughout the make-up of any window treatment. Before committing yourself to any one design, there are several points to consider when measuring for curtains. First of all, make several measurements at the same window as it will often vary slightly across the width or height because of uneven floors. Then consider the length and width of the dressing, and whether you want them to be lined or unlined.

Length Always allow for turnings and hems at the top and bottom and at the sides. This can vary according to the window treatment (see below) but recommended allowances are mentioned in each project.

Floor-length curtains often look best but sill-length curtains may be a more practical consideration in a kitchen or bathroom. Likewise, smaller windows can sometimes be swamped with floor-length curtains. For curtains that drape onto the floor, add 5-10cm/2-4in to the finished length for the hem, and then subtract 6mm/^{1}/$_4$in from the measurement to avoid draping the fabric on the ground.

For curtains hung from a pole, measure from the base of the curtain ring. But for curtains hung from a track, make an allowance for the heading so that the track will not be exposed when the curtains are closed. Add a further few centimetres/inches for the top edge of the curtain so that it stands above the track.

For blinds, measure the finished length from the top edge of the batten or pelmet board and allow for the depth of the touch-and-close fastening if this is to be run along the top of the batten or board. Alternatively, the fastening can be fixed to the front edge of the batten or board and so the length is calculated from the top edge of this.

Width Curtains can extend beyond the window area making the window seem wider than it actually is. Housing space for the curtains is often better taken up with wall space rather than window space. To establish you basic width, measure the length of the pole or track allowing for any returns, and allowing 7.5cm/3in for an overlap where the curtains meet at the middle.

Unlined curtains Many of the projects outlined in the book require a simple curtain construction. An unlined curtain is the simplest of all window coverings, and is ideal for the inexperienced sewer. The instructions that follow outline the steps you should follow to make an unlined curtain.

Measure the length of the curtain, adding 10cm/4in to the finished length for the hem. Also add 25cm/10in for a 12.5cm/5in heading, or 15cm/6in for a 7.5cm/3in heading.

Cut the fabric drops, allowing for any pattern repeat (this will always be given on the printed edge of the fabric selvage). Join the fabric lengths using a flat seam, matching the pattern if appropriate. Turn in a double seam for the sides, pin and slipstitch, or use a straight stitch on a sewing machine. Turn up the hem, once again using a double hem. Turn over the top heading and lay the heading tape along this edge. For narrow headings set the tape approximately 5cm/2in down from the top edge. For a wider tape, the heading should be set just 6mm/^{1}/$_4$in. Pin the heading and stitch in place. Ensure that the rows of stitching start from the same edge of the curtain heading to avoid any gathering of the fabric on the right side. Trap one side of the curtain heading cords with a line of stitches and then pull the cords from the other side to gather up the heading to the required width.

Pull up the heading cords to the required finished width, loop up the excess tape and tie into a neat bundle or loop this around a purchased cord tidy. Even out the gathers at the front of the curtain using your fingers. This can be done partially when the curtains are not fixed up at the window and their final adjustment is made when the curtain is on its track and they are drawn closed.

Lined curtains Often lined curtains offer a good covering for most windows. They block more light that unlined ones, hang more substantially and offer a protection against any drafts.

Measure the length of the curtain, adding the required seam and hem allowances. The length of the main (face) fabric should have 15cm/6in added for the hem and 7.5cm/3in for the turnings at the top of the curtain. Cut the lining to the finished measurement plus 10cm/4in for the hem and 2.5cm/1in for the top turning.

The width of the curtain should be two-and-a-half times the width of the finished curtain for the correct amount of fullness. Add 7.5cm/3in for the side turnings of the face fabric and 5cm/2in for the side turnings of the lining.

Cut the fabric drops, allowing for the pattern repeat and join the pieces together using a straight stitch on the sewing machine. Press the seams open. Turn over a double hem on the lining fabric and sew a line of stitches close to this fold.

Turn over 4cm/1½in side allowances on the face fabric and hand stitch in place, using a small herringbone stitch. Finish the two lines of side allowance stitches, 25cm/10in from the top and bottom of the curtain. Turn up a double 7.5cm/3in hem and mitre the corners. Hand stitch the hem.

Lay the lining over the face fabric so the hem of the lining lies 2.5cm/1in above that of the finished curtain. Turn in the edge of the lining 2.5cm/1in from the edge of the curtain and stitch. Fold the lining back on itself along every seam line and half width and lock the lining to the face fabric by hand sewing along this fold from top to

bottom. At the other side turn the lining in as for the previous side, and stitch 2.5cm/1in from the edge.

Trim the top edge of both the lining fabric and the face fabric so they are aligned. Turn over 2.5cm/1in, lay over the gathering tape, pin and stitch in position.

If you are using a narrow 2.5cm/1in heading tape, place it at least 5cm/2in down from the top edge, so that a small frill will form across the heading when the tapes are gathered. All other tapes can be stitched 12mm/½in from the top edge of the curtain.

Pull up the cords in the heading tape to the required width and tease the gathers with your fingers to even them out; when the curtain is hung from the track or pole the gathers may be further adjusted. Tie the cords into a neat bundle or around a cord tidy, and insert the curtain hooks into the heading tape.

Hanging window dressings

Pelmets are made from plywood, MDF (medium density fibreboard) or buckram and the detailed step-by-steps in this book outline pelmets using all of these materials. Once the pelmet has been constructed it should be secured above the window frame and usually there will be a curtain or perhaps a simple blind hung underneath. A pelmet board or batten will hold the pelmet at the required height and distance from the wall.

Most blinds will hang from 5 x 5cm/ 2 x 2in wooden battens which can be screwed into the wall or ceiling. Pelmet boards are usually only lengths of ordinary wood fixed above the window using right-angled brackets. These should be fixed to the wall in the same manner as a bookshelf.

CHAPTER 1

Headings
and Hems

This chapter is full of wonderful ideas for adapting an existing pair of curtains or making up new ones. The variety of headings and hems is enormous. We frequently disregard the top and bottom of a curtain or blind, but a few changes to these can often bring a new lease of life to your tired old window dressing. A smock heading could easily replace an ordinary gathered heading at little expense but can completely alter the character of your curtains. For those people who are happy with their curtains but feel they would like to add a little extra something, why not follow the lead of some of the country's best designers and stitch a corded heading onto your existing curtains? Twist upholstery cord around the regular heading, hold it with pins and a little fabric glue, then secure it with a few stitches. It really can be that easy.

Buttonhole Pelmet

If your curtains lack interest or are in need of a lift, this pretty
pelmet idea is quick and simple to make.

MATERIALS

main fabric	pins
tape measure	buttonhole fabric
scissors	needle
sewing machine	brass rings
thread	brass hooks

Hints

The clever knotting at the sides of this pelmet make it very simple to remove for cleaning.
To attach the pelmet, you will need a simple brass ring screwed at each end of the window,
2.5cm/1in or so from the top of the frame.

1 Cut a rectangle from a double thickness
of fabric. The width measures one-and-
half-times the window's width, and the drop
should be a quarter to a fifth of the window
height. Allow 2.5cm/1in for turnings. With
right sides together, stitch three sides, turn
the right sides out and stitch the gap closed.

2 Sew small pieces of contrasting fabric
5 x 7.5cm/2 x 3in onto the wrong side
of the pelmet only a fraction below the top
hem, and approximately 15cm/6in apart.
Sew a buttonhole in the centre of each
rectangle and snip through all thicknesses.
Push the fabric through the hole.

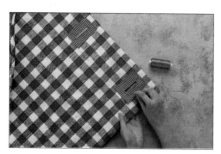

3 On the right side, hand sew the raw
edges under on all four sides of the
buttonhole facing. Make tiny stitches using
a similarly coloured thread. You may need
to tug the fabric slightly to stop the fabric
bunching up at the top and bottom of the
buttonhole. If this does not work you may
need to re-snip the buttonhole.

4 Cut the tie from a double thickness of
fabric, and along the fabric fold. The
depth of the tie is 4cm/1 $\frac{1}{2}$in and the length
equals the pelmet. Allow 2.5cm/1in for
turnings. With right sides facing, sew along
one end and the long side. Turn right sides
out and stitch the open edge closed. Press
flat, thread through the pelmet and tie.

Twisted Cord
Heading

This heading can be applied to
new or existing curtains as you
wish. Try twisting the rope into a
variety of shapes and coils.

MATERIALS

string

cord

pins

fabric glue

needle

thread

scissors

Hints

If you are sewing the cord onto your
existing curtains, you need not necessarily
remove them from the track - provided you
can sew while you are up a ladder! But
remember to close the curtains before
stitching the cord in place.

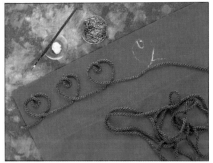

1 To establish how much cord you need to buy, first decide on the type of twist you would like on a table top using a piece of string. Then, still using the string, repeat the twist along the curtain heading and buy the necessary amount of cord. Practise coiling the cord and then twist it onto the curtain heading, and pin securely. Glue the cord once the position is right.

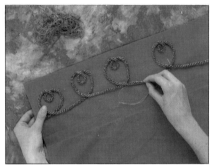

2 Once the glue has dried, start to sew the twisted cord in position. You will need to hand stitch this in place using a similar coloured thread. Once the stitching is complete, remove the pins. Sew the ends of the cord to the back of the curtain.

Black and White Curtain Heading

Monochromatic colours can look stunning at a window, particularly if the drapes are long. This particular heading is designed to hang from a curtain pole.

MATERIALS

string

ribbon

iron and ironing board

pins

needle

thread

scissors

curtain fabric

cloth

fringed edge

rickrack braid

fabric glue

Hints

Any soft fringe can be used under this checked ribbon heading. Browse around the trimming department in your local department store for inspiration. If your favourite trimming isn't available in black you may be able to dye it if it is 100 per cent cotton.

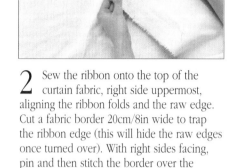

1 Zigzag a piece of string above your curtain heading in the same way as the intended ribbon edging. This will give you the exact length of ribbon to buy. Fold the ribbon in zigzags and use a warm iron to press the folds. You may find it easier to work on the ironing board, pinning the folds as you go.

2 Sew the ribbon onto the top of the curtain fabric, right side uppermost, aligning the ribbon folds and the raw edge. Cut a fabric border 20cm/8in wide to trap the ribbon edge (this will hide the raw edges once turned over). With right sides facing, pin and then stitch the border over the zigzag ribbon 12mm/$^{1}/_{2}$in from the edge.

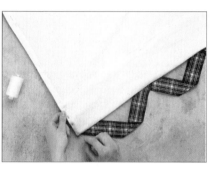

3 Turn the border over to reveal the ribbons, tug them to make sure they lie flat and press the heading. Sew a narrow hem along the length of the border to hide the raw edges and then sew a narrow hem down the length of each curtain, trapping the border fabric into the seam. Protect the ribbon edge with a damp cloth before using a hot iron to press it.

4 Hand stitch a fringe edging onto the front of the curtain, aligning the edge of the tape with the top edge of the curtain. Use a complementary colour of thread (here, of course I used black) and make tiny, invisible stitches.

5 As a final decorative flourish, add a length of white rickrack braid over the black fringe. Glue it over the top edge of the fringe and then use invisible stitches to secure the braid firmly in place.

Crown Heading

Tired of looking at conventional curtain headings? This unique, pointed heading certainly adds a flourish to the top of any curtain.

Hints

This bright fabric would add a splash of colour to a child's room or a nursery, or simply substitute a natural, creamy-coloured fabric for an up-to-the-minute look for a living room or bedroom.

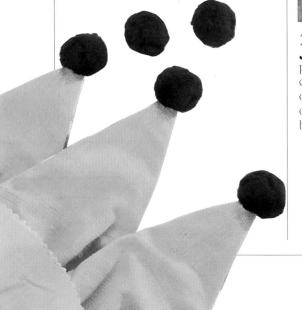

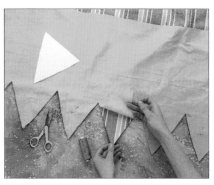

1 Measure your window carefully and follow the guidelines in the introduction for making up a simple unlined curtain. As this curtain is not lined, cut a piece of backing fabric to cover the pointed edge and extend below any tape or gathering lines. To make sure the points remain consistent, cut a paper template and use this to cut out the main and backing fabrics at the same time. Pin together with right sides facing.

2 Stitch around the heading. For a continuous stitching line, stop the machine at the top and bottom of each point, making sure the needle is through all thicknesses of fabric. Then lift the foot, turn the fabric, replace the foot and continue. Clip into the points and turn the heading to the right side.

3 For a decorative flourish you may wish to sew little pompoms on top of each point. These can be bought at craft or department stores, but if you have difficulty obtaining them, you could make your own or choose an alternative, such as beads or buttons.

4 Turn the fabric over to the reverse side and pin then stitch a standard curtain heading tape just below the pointed heading. Stitch over the ends and use the cords to gather up the heading. Tug each point gently and slip curtain hooks into the gathered tape to hang the curtain.

Flower Button Heading

These jewel-like buttons are eye-catching on a curtain heading, particularly if you sew them onto bright-coloured curtain fabric as I have done, with brightly contrasting looped ties.

MATERIALS

tracing paper

paper

pencil

scissors

coloured felt

patterned fabrics

self-cover buttons

thread

needle

fabric for ties

fabric glue

curtain fabric

iron and ironing board

Hints

For a more sophisticated flower heading make each flower using the same two fabrics. Use only one colour of felt to make the petals (coordinate it with the curtain fabric), and a second fabric for the centres of each flower.

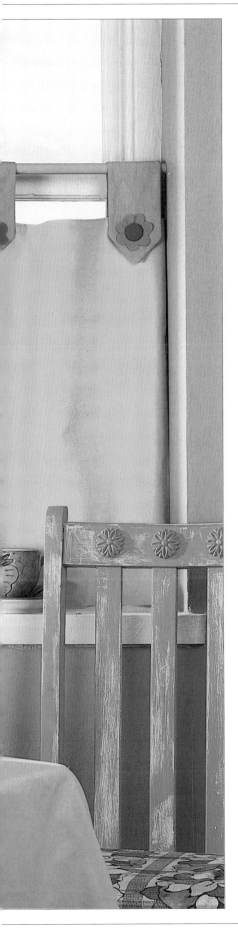

1 Trace around the flower template on this page and enlarge on a photocopier to an appropriate size. Use the outline to cut out felt petals. Also cut out squares of patterned fabric. Sew around the edges with small running stitches, and pull up the threads, enclosing the top half of a self-cover button. Press the two button halves together, trapping the felt petals in between.

2 For each tie, cut long thin rectangles 7.5 x 25cm/3 x 10in from a double thickness of fabric and cut a pointed end. With right sides facing, sew around three sides and turn right sides out. Cut a small contrasting 2.5 x 5cm/1 x 2in piece of fabric, pin it above the point on the tie and sew a buttonhole on top.

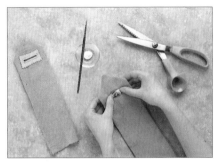

3 Turn the buttonhole fabric through to the other side of the tie. To neaten, sew around the edge of the buttonhole and stick down the excess fabric with a little fabric glue for added security. You will need one tie approximately every 30cm/12in; repeat the same process as above for each tie.

4 Place each tie onto the front of the curtain fabric with the points facing downwards and the raw fabric edges of the buttonhole to the inside. As the curtain is not lined, sew a fabric backing panel over the ties, right sides facing, through all thicknesses and down the two sides. This traps the ties and neatens the whole curtain.

5 Turn the fabric to the right side and tug each tie to straighten. Press the curtain using a damp cloth to flatten the seams. Sew a flower button beneath each tie 2.5cm/1in from the top edge. The tie is designed to loop over a curtain pole and fasten around each flower button.

Eyelet Pull-up
Blind

This has to be the quickest
and easiest of window coverings
yet, nevertheless it looks stylish
and original.

MATERIALS

blind fabric

lining fabric (optional)

tape measure

thread

touch-and-close fastener

cord

eyelets and punch

hammer

small fabric pieces

wooden batten (5 x 2.5cm/2 x 1in)

screws

screwdriver

tacks

Hints

If you are looking for a blind to block
the light you will need to sew a lining
onto the face fabric. Cut out the face fabric
and the lining fabric to the same size but
trim 10cm/4in from the width of the lining
fabric. Sew the pieces together, stitching
down the sides, and turn to the right sides
and press. The broader face fabric will
form a natural border along the two inside
edges of the blind.

1 Cut the face fabric to size, allowing 2.5cm/1in for side turnings and 30cm/12in for top and bottom turnings. Fold these turnings under twice to enclose the raw edges and stitch down. Sew one half of a touch-and-close fastener across the top hem, trapping a length of cord, each the same length as the blind drop, into the fastener 20cm/8in in from each side seam.

2 Punch a row of eyelets down each side of the blind, keeping them 20cm/8in from each side of the blind. The eyelets should be 20cm/8in apart but always punch an uneven number down each side. To strengthen the blind, insert a piece of fabric between the two parts of each eyelet and on the wrong side of the face fabric prior to punching.

3 Thread the cord up through the first eyelet and down through the second and so on until both sides have been threaded. Attach the other half of the touch-and-close fastener to a batten above the window and secure the blind onto this. You may need a few tacks as well as the touch-and-close fastener for security. Tie the cords at the required height.

Velvet Roses Heading

These attractive roses are twisted into shape and sewn at the back to secure. They are then sewn directly onto an existing curtain, or onto new curtains as you prefer.

MATERIALS

velvet fabric (2 colours)

tape measure

thread

scissors

needle

Hints

Don't be tempted to sew the roses onto your curtains without removing them from the curtain track first. Sewing from the top of a ladder may be all right for the first couple of roses, but your arms will soon get tired.

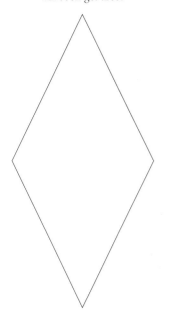

1 For each rose, cut a 23 x 15cm/9 x 6in rectangle from a piece of velvet, and fold in half lengthways with wrong sides facing. Stitch the long seam closed. Start to roll up the rectangle from left to right, twisting the fabric slightly as you progress to bunch up the velvet. Secure the rose with several long stitches at its base.

2 Trace the leaf outline from this page and enlarge on a photocopier to an appropriate size. Cut a paper template from the outline and then cut the leaves from a double thickness of green velvet, adding a 12mm/$\frac{1}{2}$in seam allowance. With right sides together, stitch around the leaves, leaving a small gap. Turn the right side out and hand stitch the gap closed. Gather the middle of the leaf and stitch behind each rose.

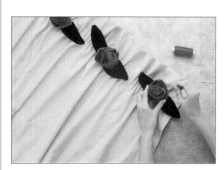

3 If you are using existing curtains, remove them from their track and position the velvet roses along the headings. Secure the roses to the curtains over the gathering tape using long stitches. Make sure that the stitches are hidden inside the folds of velvet. The roses must be detached from the curtains before cleaning.

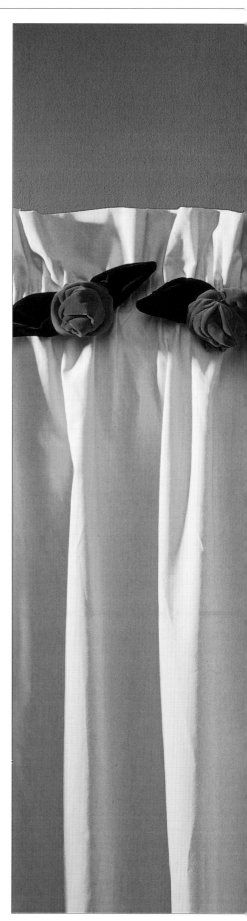

Seashore Wave Hem

Here I show you how to sew this detailed edge to a basic unlined curtain, but you could add the wave detail to the hem of an existing curtain or soft fabric blind, provided you remove the lining temporarily.

MATERIALS

tape measure

fabric (2 colours)

scissors

pins

thread

sewing machine

tailor's chalk

embroiderer's scissors

Hints

Although these primary colours would suit a child's room, this wave edging also looks good in a living room when different colours are used. A black wave looks stunning against creamy damask.

Choose two fabrics that have compatible cleaning methods, and make sure that the colours are fast, so they do not run in the wash.

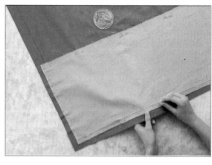

1 If you are sewing a curtain specifically for this edging, measure your window carefully and follow the guidelines in the introduction for making up a simple unlined curtain. Turn over a double seam allowance to conceal any raw edges, pin and stitch.

2 Pin a strip of contrasting fabric to the reverse of the curtain directly over the area where the seashore wave is to be stitched. The right side of the contrasting fabric should be facing the wrong side of the main fabric.

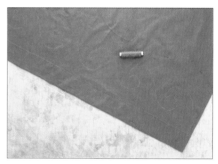

3 Trace the outline supplied on this page and enlarge the design on a photocopier to an appropriate size. Using tailor's chalk, draw a faint line on the right side of the fabric where you want the wave's base line to fall. Then place the bottom edge of the paper template against this and draw on the wave border.

4 Use a thread that matches the colour of one of the fabrics, and select a running stitch on your sewing machine. Carefully stitch around the wave edge, keeping the fabric as flat as possible. To stitch neat waves, stop at the crest of each one with the needle down through the fabric and then lift the sewing foot and turn the fabric.

5 Use sharp scissors to cut through the top layer of fabric only, slowly working around the line of stitches. Turn the fabric over and cut up to the stitching line to remove excess fabric from the back of the curtain. This leaves a neat wave edge on both sides of the curtain.

Smocked
Heading

This heading is certainly
eye-catching. Although the
smocking can be done by hand,
you can now buy specially
produced smocked heading tape
which gives you guaranteed
results in a fraction of the time.

MATERIALS

curtain fabric

tape measure

scissors

smocked tape heading

thread

needle

beads (optional)

Hints

Only use this smocked heading on a curtain
where the gathered heading is fixed on the
track. The curtain is held back at the sides,
allowing the attractive heading to be seen at
all times.

1 Measure your window carefully and follow the guidelines in the introduction for making up a simple unlined curtain. Turn over double side seams to conceal any raw edges, and turn over deeper hems across the top and bottom. Machine stitch the heading over the top hem, leaving a 5cm/2in gap between the heading tape and the top of the curtain.

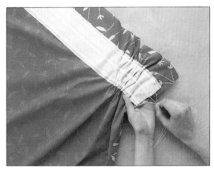

2 Across the leading edge of the curtain, stitch a double row of stitches to trap the three lines of heading tape cords. Make sure that they stay free on the outer edge. Hold the heading tape taut while you are stitching to avoid any gathering on the front. Pull the cords to the required width.

3 Even out the gathers on the right side of the curtain to form a regularly spaced heading. Gently tug the top and bottom of the heading and you will see that it forms the characteristic smocked heading. For a pretty effect, sew a small bead at each point that the folds meet.

Tied Curtain Heading

On this curtain, the gathering tape has been dyed to coordinate with the patterned fabric. This is then sewn onto the front of the curtain as part of the decorative treatment.

MATERIALS

curtain fabric

tape measure

scissors

fabric dye

heading tape

pins

ribbon

thread

sewing machine

Hints

Use a good-quality cotton heading tape for dying; synthetic materials will not take to the dye as well as natural fibres. Natural cotton ribbon may also be dyed to match rather than purchasing coloured ribbon. Follow the manufacturer's instructions when dying the tape or ribbon.

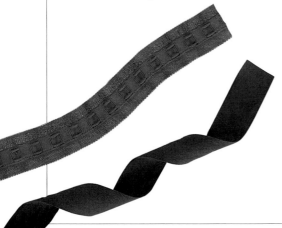

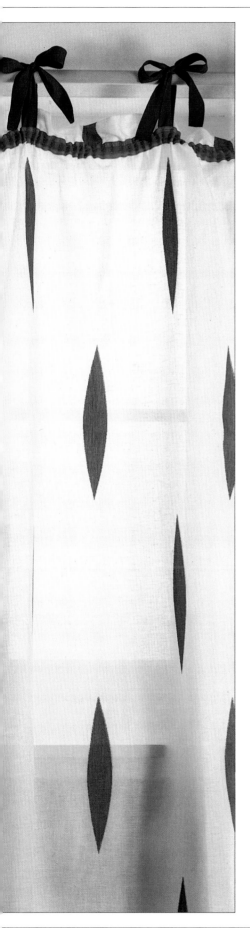

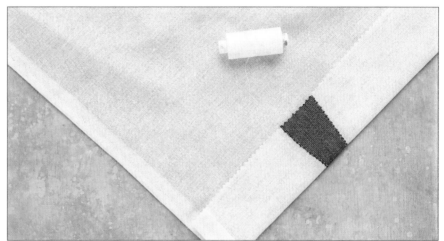

1 Measure your window carefully and follow the guidelines in the introduction for making up a simple unlined curtain. This type of heading would also suit a simple lined curtain, provided the overall effect is softly unstructured. This would be ideal for most country-style homes in living rooms and bedrooms alike.

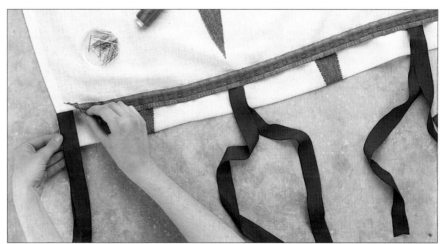

2 Pin the dyed heading tape in place leaving a gap of approximately 5cm/2in between the top of the curtain and the tape to produce a softly frilled heading that will flop over the tape. Cut 35.5cm/14in lengths of ribbon, fold in half and insert into the top of the heading at regular intervals of 25cm/10in. Stitch the heading tape in place, trapping the ribbons as you sew. Start stitching the heading tape by sewing across the heading cords at the leading edge of each curtain. Make sure the cords stay free on the outer edge. Then stitch from one end of the tape to the other, trapping the ribbons as you sew. Finally, start from the same end to stitch the lower edge of the tape. Hold the heading tape taut while you are stitching to avoid any gathering on the front of the curtain.

Cut-out Leaf Heading

This curtaining idea looks very effective with natural light filtering through the muslin leaves, so it is important to have a fixed heading like the one I have used here. The curtain is then scooped back at the sides and held in place with a simple holdback.

MATERIALS

fabric for curtaining

tape measure

scissors

pins

muslin

sewing machine

thread

tracing paper

pencil

paper

embroiderer's scissors

Hints

Unpatterned fabrics are most effective for this window treatment. Bear in mind that the curtains should be left unlined for the light to show through.

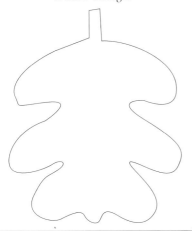

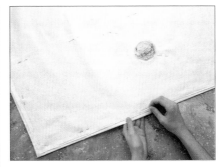

1 Measure your window carefully and follow the guidelines in the introduction for making up a simple unlined curtain. Place the curtain on a flat surface, wrong side uppermost and pin a deep muslin border over the area where the leaf motifs are to be stitched.

2 Trace the leaf motif on this page and enlarge it on a photocopier to an appropriate size. Cut out the leaf and use this as a template. Determine how many leaf shapes you will need across the heading by measuring and then marking their positions on the right side of the fabric with a pencil. Place the template over each mark and draw around the shape.

3 Use a close zigzag stitch on your machine to sew around the edges of the leaf, turning the fabric carefully as you stitch to maintain an even line. Keep the fabric taut to avoid unnecessary gathers. Snip away the fabric, close to the sewn edge at the front and back of the curtain, as for the Seashore Wave Hem on page 28.

Canvas Fringed Curtain

A simple fringe sewn down the edge of a curtain can transform a plain, uninteresting fabric. A line of detailed embroidery stitched down the sides of the fringe gives a pretty finishing touch.

MATERIALS

loose weave fabric

sewing machine

scissors

thread

Hints

Most basic sewing machines will be able to sew a line of embroidery-type stitches. Select a zigzag stitch with a close width to sew an edge as I have done here, or hand stitch a border if you prefer.

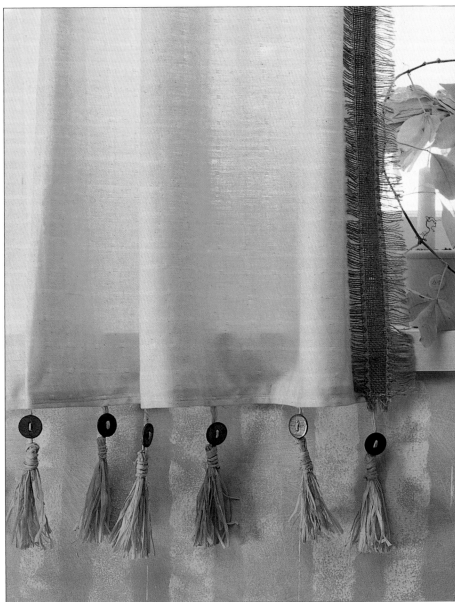

1 For the fringe, select a fabric that is loosely woven so the threads can be pulled away easily. Cut the fabric into sufficiently long thin strips, approximately 7.5cm/3in wide, to cover both sides of the curtain. Start to pull threads from the strips using your thumb and forefinger.

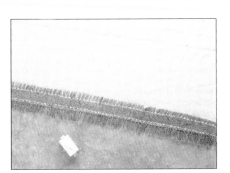

2 When the fringed threads are almost long enough, use a sewing machine to stitch the embroidery down both sides of each strip. Use the fringed sides as a guide to keep the stitches as straight as possible. When the embroidery is complete, pull a few more threads to meet the stitching line. Sew onto the edges of your curtain.

Raffia Tassels

These tassels are effective for weighting the hem of a curtain, particularly if your curtain is not lined or is made from a lightweight fabric.

MATERIALS

raffia

scissors

large needle

metal weighted buttons

Hints

These metal buttons, traditionally used as weights for curtains, are normally placed inside the hem. Here, their attractive, pewter-like appearance is displayed on the outside.

1 For each tassel, cut approximately ten lengths of raffia and tie them together securely across the middle using another piece of raffia. Fold the bundle in half across the middle and use a further raffia strip to bind the top of the tassel. Tie the binding securely and snip any untidy ends.

2 Thread a large needle with two more strands of raffia and sew them onto the top of each tassel. Then sew a button onto the top of each tassel, passing the raffia through the two button holes.

3 Use a thin piece of raffia to stitch the tassel to the curtain hem and trim away any excess. Repeat as many times as you need.

CHAPTER 2

Tiebacks and Holdbacks

When you think of tiebacks I expect what usually springs to mind is the crescent-shaped variety made to coordinate with the curtain fabric. Well, think again. Delightful rag dolls made from fabric scraps can be joined together to form a circle of dancing dolls around a nursery window, a simply stitched appliqué pocket can be sewn into a tieback and filled with scented lavender or pot pourri. These are just some of the ideas you can follow to add a touch of originality to your interior. Holdbacks too are the perfect accessories to decorate, and it is easy to transform purchased mundane examples into glorious felt sunflowers or gilded stars. It doesn't take a huge amount of fabric to make a tieback or decorate a holdback, so you could afford to use some of the exquisite fabrics that you may normally have to avoid.

Appliqué Pocket Tiebacks

Not only do these tiebacks look
pretty, they are functional as well.
Use the little pocket to store
potpourri, or to hold small
bunches of sweet-smelling
lavender.

MATERIALS

various fabrics

scissors

self-cover buttons

needle and thread

beads

tracing paper

pencil

paper

sewing machine

string

fusible interfacing

brass rings

brass hooks

Hints

Tie the potpourri fragrance inside a small
fabric bag so that it can be easily replaced
when the fragrance has worn away. Do not
top up the fragrance with scented oils as
they may seep into the fabric.

1 For each tieback, cut a small circle of fabric wide enough to place over the self-cover button and sew tiny beads over the fabric to decorate it. Lay the beaded fabric over the top half of the button and tuck the raw edges to the inside. Place the second half over this and snap the two pieces together.

2 Cut out two pieces of fabric for the pocket back (17 x 20cm/6$^{1}/_{2}$ x 8in) and a smaller rectangle for the pocket front (17 x 18cm/6$^{1}/_{2}$ x 6$^{3}/_{4}$in). Fold back the top of the pocket front and stitch in place. Trace the heart motif on this page and enlarge it on a photocopier to an appropriate size. Use this template to cut out a fabric heart and pin it onto the front of the pocket. Hold in place with long running stitches worked by hand.

3 Insert the pocket front between the two pieces of pocket back fabric (their right sides should be facing). Stitch the pocket pieces together along three sides. Turn right sides out and hand stitch the remaining gap closed.

4 Place a small rectangular scrap of fabric over the area at the top of the pocket flap, with right sides facing, and stitch a buttonhole over this. Cut into the buttonhole and push the excess fabric through to the wrong side.

5 Pass a piece of string around the curtain where the tieback will be and use this measurement to cut the tieback, following the instructions outlined for the buttonhole tieback overleaf. For a stiffer tieback, include a layer of fusible interfacing between the two layers of fabric.

6 Stitch the two fabric pieces together with right sides facing, leaving a small gap to turn to the right side. Turn and then stitch the gap closed with small hand stitches. Sew the button in place and fix on the appliqué pocket. Sew two brass rings to the ends of each tieback.

Knotted Buttonhole Tiebacks

Tiebacks are without a doubt extremely useful. They can, however, look quite boring in their conventional form so here is a unique approach to tying back your curtains.

MATERIALS

tape measure

paper

pencil

scissors

triangle fabric

thread

sewing machine

iron and ironing board

tieback fabric

needle

brass rings

brass hooks

Hints

For more traditional curtains use the same fabric for the tiebacks as for the curtains. However, if your room warrants it, go for an eclectic look: mismatched checks or a selection of muted floral chintzes would each look exciting.

To make a template for your tiebacks, pass a cloth tape measure around your curtains at the point where the tiebacks will be to determine its length. Transfer this measurement onto paper, and then draw a crescent shape around the line using the tieback featured on this page as a guide. Cut out the resulting shape.

1 For each tieback, cut small triangles from a double thickness of fabric. Two sides of the triangle should measure 9cm/3 $^{1}/_{2}$in and the base approximately 7.5cm/3in. Stitch down the two longer sides leaving a seam allowance of 12mm/$^{1}/_{2}$in, turn the shape to the right side and press flat using a steam iron.

2 Use the paper template described in the Hints text to the left to cut two crescent shapes from the main fabric. Place them together with right sides facing and insert the triangles along the bottom edge, points facing into the crescent tieback. Stitch around the edges, leaving a seam allowance of 12mm/$^{1}/_{2}$in. Leave a small gap to turn the tieback to the right side. Stitch the gap closed.

3 Place a rectangle of fabric cut from that used for the triangles over one end of the tieback and stitch a 4cm/1 $^{1}/_{2}$in buttonhole over this. Snip the buttonhole and push the fabric through to the other side. Hand sew the buttonhole flat on the right side, and turn under the raw edges on the reverse. To attach the tiebacks onto hooks fixed to the wall, stitch a small brass ring to the centre of each tieback on the wrong side. Scoop each curtain into a tieback and slip the tie through the buttonhole.

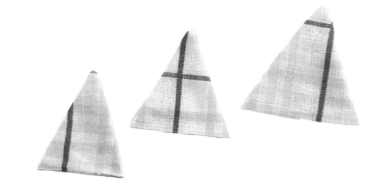

Ivy Twist
Tiebacks

A few strands of fake ivy add interest to this ingenious way of tying back ordinary curtains.

MATERIALS

tape measure

scissors

ivy fabric

lining fabric

thread

needle

plastic-coated garden wire

fusible webbing

iron and ironing board

fabric glue (optional)

sewing machine

brass rings

brass hooks

Hints

Use plastic-coated wire to stitch inside the tiebacks, or look for wire that will not rust in the wash.

1 Pass a cloth tape measure around your curtains at the point where the tiebacks will be to determine the length of your ivy twist. For each tieback, cut out a strip of ivy fabric and the lining fabric to this size, and hand stitch a length of wire to the reverse side of the ivy fabric, following its stem. Bend the wire into a small loop at either end to prevent the wire from sliding through the stitches.

2 Use fusible webbing and an iron to fix the lining fabric to the printed fabric, and then trim both the backing fabric and fusible webbing to match the facing fabric. If you have difficulty obtaining fusible webbing, a little fabric glue should be sufficient to bond the two fabric pieces together while you stitch around the edges.

3 Use a close zigzag stitch on your machine to stitch around the edges of the twist. Keep the fabric taut as you stitch, turning the fabric under the sewing foot as you go. For each tieback, sew a brass ring in the centre of the lining fabric and fasten it onto a hook. Finally, twist the tiebacks around the curtains.

Rag Doll Tiebacks

These delightful dolls are joined together with touch-and-close fastener which means they can be removed for play or cleaning at any time.

MATERIALS

tracing paper	trimmings
pencil	beads
paper	buttons
scissors	wool yarn
fabric pieces	needle
felt pieces (pink, brown, red)	thread
fabric glue	touch-and-close fastener

Hints

Use the touch-and-close fastener on the dolls' hands to attach them to the curtains as well as to make the tiebacks. The dolls can also be separated from each other and replaced in different positions.

1 Trace the template on this page and enlarge it on a photocopier to an appropriate size. Use the template to cut out a fabric backing for each doll, a dress and pink or brown felt faces. Use different fabrics for each doll. Apply fabric glue over the backing and stick on the dress and face.

2 Decorate the dresses with colourful spots or hearts and flowers all cut from coloured fabric. Use fabric glue to stick them in place. Also stick on whatever decorative trimmings catch your eye: beads or buttons look good, and rickrack braid and pompom edgings look pretty along the hems.

3 Use strands of wool yarn for the hair; a few stitches will hold these in place. Stitch on tiny beads for the eyes and glue on a pair of red felt lips. Make each doll as individual as you can; use yellow, black and red wool yarn for the hair, cutting both long and short strands. Plait strands if you wish.

4 Attach touch-and-close fastener to the dolls' arms to link them together. Two loops of dolls fastened over a hook on either side of each curtain will hold them back. When the curtains are closed the loops may be joined together to form a line of dolls across them.

Appliqué Heart Holdbacks

These holdbacks are positioned at the top of a window frame and are used to hold a decorative swag of fabric.

MATERIALS

self-cover holdbacks

main fabric

tracing paper

pencil

paper

scissors

fabric pieces

thread

needle

beads

embroidery thread

Hints

These self-cover holdbacks are perfect for making your own, but if you have difficulty obtaining them you could make them using a circle of wood and a short length of dowelling. Screw the dowelling into the wall using a double-ended screw and glue the circle of wood to the end.

1 For each holdback, cut the main fabric to size using the button holdback as a guide and remembering to leave enough fabric to pull around to the inside of the button. Make a heart template as on page 40 and cut the heart shape from a small piece of cloth. Position it centrally onto the circle of fabric and sew tiny beads onto the heart.

2 Use long, overstated stitches and a bright-coloured embroidery thread to stitch a naive edging around the heart. I used an orange thread to coordinate with the rich colours of my fabrics but you could use a contrasting blue or purple thread with equally successful results.

3 Place the appliqué over the self-cover button, aligning the centre of the button with the centre of the heart. Pull the excess fabric around to the reverse side and place the back of the button over this. Snap the two pieces together to secure. Twist in the stem support and position it.

Cummerbund Tiebacks

The style of this tieback reminds me of the tailored waistbands that stylish men often wear with dinner jackets. So it is with a little amusement that I find myself holding a pair of curtains back with them.

MATERIALS

tape measure

paper

pencil

scissors

main fabric

lining fabric

buckram (optional)

buttons

thread

needle

iron and ironing board

brass rings

brass hooks

Hints

Look for coordinating fabrics such as these in remnant bins. The top fabric here has delicate embroidery stripes running across it which look perfect for this holdback, but you could use a striped fabric with similar results; even striped shirt fabric would look good. If you are using a lightweight fabric you may wish to add a layer of buckram for support.

1 Pass a cloth tape measure around your curtains at the point where the tieback will be to determine its length and transfer this measurement onto a piece of paper. Dissect this line in the centre with an 18cm/7in long line (9cm/3 ¹⁄₂in on either side), and add 5cm/2in long lines - again centred - at each end. Then connect the points with curved lines to produce a template for the tieback. For each tieback, cut out two pieces of each fabric.

2 Sew buttons down the centre of each top piece. Sew the front and back of the tieback together, right sides facing, leaving a seam allowance of 12mm/¹⁄₂in. Leave a small gap open in order to turn the fabric to the right side. Stitch the gap closed with tiny hand stitches. Press the fabric carefully.

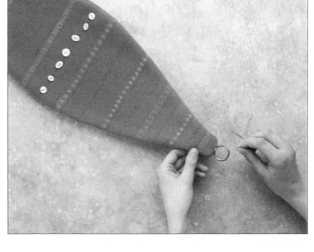

3 Sew a small brass ring to each end of each tieback and use these to fasten the tiebacks onto hooks screwed into the wall at the sides of the curtains. Scoop the fabric back and arrange the folds neatly inside each tieback. To close the curtains, unfasten one ring from the hook.

Gilded Star Holdbacks

These attractive star shapes are sawn from pieces of plywood or medium-density fibreboard (MDF) using a fret saw. Less expensive Dutch metal leaf is used instead of real gold leaf.

MATERIALS

tracing paper

pencil

paper

scissors

plywood or MDF

fret saw

gesso (or acrylic paint)

small paintbrush

PVA adhesive

Dutch metal leaf (or gold paint)

acrylic varnish

sandpaper or wire wool

dowelling

wood glue

double-ended screws

Hints

When using the fret saw, cut down and along each point of the star, stopping the saw at the base of each point. Then start at the top again rather than trying to turn the corner and saw up the side of a point.

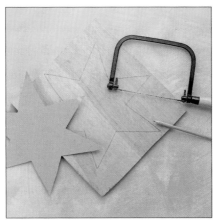

1 Trace the diagram on this page and enlarge it on a photocopier to a suitable size. Cut the star from the paper and use this as a template to draw around. You will need two stars, one for each side of the window. Cut the shape carefully from plywood or MDF.

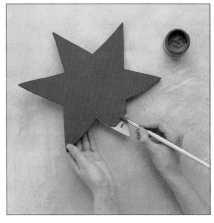

2 For each star, paint the front and back with a coat of red gesso. This product looks particularly good under the gilded surface when it is distressed as its colour is very attractive. If you have difficulty obtaining it you could use acrylic paint in a similar colour.

3 Apply a thin layer of PVA adhesive over the stars and leave it until almost dry; it should be just tacky. Press a sheet of Dutch metal leaf onto the surface, applying enough sheets to cover the stars' surface. Press the transfer sheet with a dry brush to make sure there is good contact. Rub away excess leaf and varnish the surface to protect it.

4 When the metal leaf is thoroughly dry, use a piece of sandpaper or a little wire wool to distress the surface slightly, allowing a little of the base colour to show through. Attach a length of dowelling to each star with wood glue, and in turn attach the holdbacks to the wall using double-ended screws.

Sunflower Holdbacks

These attractive holdbacks look particularly good with lightweight cotton or muslin fabrics.

MATERIALS

self-cover holdback

brown felt

scissors

tracing paper

pencil

paper

yellow felt

black felt

fabric glue

beads

thread

needle

black wool yarn

Hints

Bright-coloured felt is the best material for the sunflower petals; most other fabrics would fray when cut.

1 Using the top half of the self-cover button as a guide and for each holdback, cut a circle from the brown felt to make the centre of the sunflower. Enlarge the petal outline on this page on a photocopier to an appropriate size, and use this as a template to cut out the yellow felt petals. Glue tiny circles of black felt onto the brown felt circle.

2 To add further interest to the centre of the flower, sew tiny black beads between the black felt circles, and also stitch French knots of black wool yarn for extra texture. If you have small children it may be advisable to secure the black felt spots with a stitch or two to prevent them from being pulled off.

3 Cover the self-cover button with the sunflower centre, folding over the excess felt. Place the yellow petals over the back of the button and press the two halves together. Screw the fixings to the base of the holdbacks and attach them to your wall.

Plaited Tiebacks

These tiebacks are made up from old sweaters that have been felted in a hot wash. They were then cut into strips and plaited tightly together to form a thick, soft band.

MATERIALS

knitwear

scissors

tape measure

thread

needle

brass rings

brass hooks

Hints

Select knitted items that are variations of the same colour. You can often find woollen jumpers in secondhand shops that have been shrunk in a too hot wash. Lambswool produces the best effect; it is perfect for plaiting.

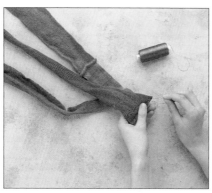

1 Wash your selection of knitwear in a hot wash to felt the wool. Dry and then cut long strips from the fabric - the length of the strips equals the finished length of the tiebacks plus 7.5cm/3in. For each tieback, sew three strips together at the top and plait to make one strand. Repeat twice, making three similar strands in all.

2 Using tiny hand stitches, sew two plaits together down their length. Then sew the third plait to this larger plait in the same way to form the triple plait. If you want a wider strip, simply keep adding more plaits until you have the required width.

3 Sew a brass ring to each end of the tiebacks. Slip one ring over the hooks screwed into the wall at the sides of the window and fold the curtains back into each tieback. Pass the second rings over the hooks to hold the curtains. To release the curtains, simply undo the top rings.

Beaded
Holdbacks

These jewelled holdbacks look
good around a pair of curtains
at a conventional dado height.

MATERIALS

self-cover holdback

fabric pieces

translucent fabric

scissors

pencil

beads

thread

needle

Hints

To make a guide for stitching on the
tiny beads, place a self-cover holdback
on each circle of fabric and draw
a pencil line lightly around its
circumference. Sew on the beads
within this line.

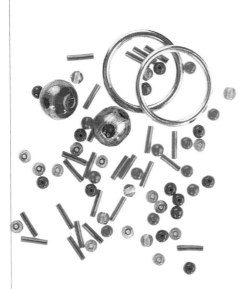

1 For each holdback, cut a fabric circle
using the self-cover holdback as a
guide, remembering to leave sufficient
allowance for drawing-up the fabric beneath
the button. Cut a layer of translucent fabric
and place this over the base fabric for a
pretty effect. Sew the beads onto the face
fabric until the base is almost covered. Make
a line of running stitches around the outside
of the circle.

2 Pull up the running stitches and slip the
cover over the holdback. Pull the
stitching thread further to fold all the raw
edges over to the back of the holdback.
Press on the second half of the holdback,
snapping the two pieces firmly together.
Screw the fixings to the base of the
holdbacks and fix into your wall.

Beaded Tiebacks

Transform plain tiebacks with a few tiny beads. These simple flower decorations look best when stitched against an unpatterned fabric.

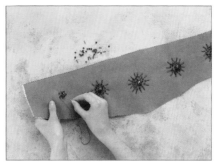

1 Pass a cloth tape measure around your curtain at the point where the tieback will be to determine its length and transfer this measurement onto a piece of paper. Draw a 15cm/6in line at the centre of this line at right angles and 7.5cm/3in lines at either end. Connect the points to make your pelmet template. For each tieback, cut a piece from the face fabric and stitch beads onto it following my example above.

2 Again using the paper template as a guide, cut a piece from the lining fabric. With right sides facing, stitch the face fabric to the lining with a seam allowance of 12mm/^{1}/2in. Leave a small gap, turn the right sides out and neatly hand stitch the gap closed.

3 Sew a small brass ring to each end of the tiebacks and use them to secure the tiebacks to the wall-mounted hooks. Pull the curtains back to the sides of the window, wrap the tiebacks around them and pass the rings over the hooks. To close the curtains, release one ring of the tiebacks and allow them to drop down.

MATERIALS

tape measure

paper

pencil

ruler

scissors

fabric for tieback

beads

thread

needle

lining for tieback

sewing machine (optional)

brass rings

brass hooks

Hints

Look for small packets of mixed beads in craft shops and department stores. A few beads go a long way.

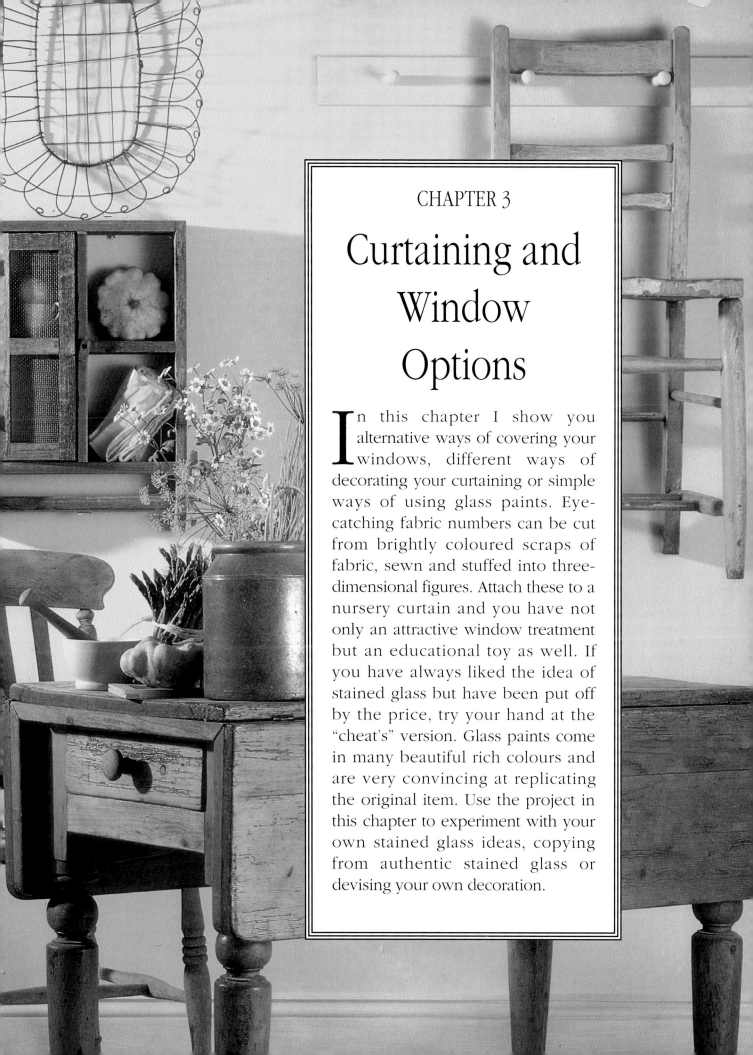

CHAPTER 3

Curtaining and Window Options

In this chapter I show you alternative ways of covering your windows, different ways of decorating your curtaining or simple ways of using glass paints. Eye-catching fabric numbers can be cut from brightly coloured scraps of fabric, sewn and stuffed into three-dimensional figures. Attach these to a nursery curtain and you have not only an attractive window treatment but an educational toy as well. If you have always liked the idea of stained glass but have been put off by the price, try your hand at the "cheat's" version. Glass paints come in many beautiful rich colours and are very convincing at replicating the original item. Use the project in this chapter to experiment with your own stained glass ideas, copying from authentic stained glass or devising your own decoration.

Dinosaur Curtain Edging

Classic gingham checks are used to great effect here to create this clever dinosaur edge for a child's room.

MATERIALS

tracing paper

pencil

paper

scissors

check fabric

gingham fabric

dotted fabric

iron and ironing board

curtain fabric

thread

sewing machine

lining fabric (optional)

Hints

This edging is created from three layers of fabric scallops - you could use fewer or more layers, depending on your time and patience! You will need to place scallops along the width of the curtain, leaving a gap of 5cm/2in between each one.

1 Trace the outline on this page and enlarge it on a photocopier to an appropriate size. Use the resulting template to cut out fabric scallop shapes from double thicknesses of fabric. With right sides facing, sew around the curved line of each shape, keeping the stitching as close to the raw edges as possible. Turn the shapes rights sides out and press.

2 Cut two 12.5cm/5in deep borders from the main fabric across its width. Place the first row of scallop shapes along one border piece and sandwich these between the second border piece, with right sides together. Stitch along the top hem leaving a small seam allowance.

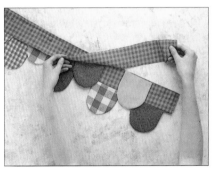

3 Fold the top and bottom border fabrics upwards and press. Fold each border strip inwards, reducing their widths by half and creating a weighted hem to the curtain. Place more scallops along the top edge of this border, positioning them over the gaps formed by the scallops beneath. Then with right sides facing, sew a half-width border (6.25cm/2 1/2in) across them.

4 Place yet another line of scallops along this top edge to produce the third layer of decoration. With right sides together, pin then stitch the bottom edge of the curtain fabric over the border. Keep the fabric taut as you feed the fabric under the sewing foot to avoid unnecessary gathers.

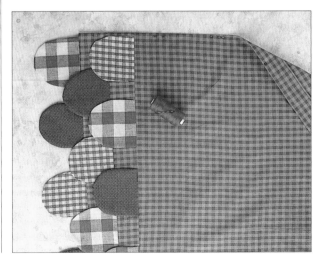

5 If you wish to make lined curtains, stitch a lining to this fabric following the instructions in the introduction. Or turn under a double hem down the side of the curtain if you wish to hang the fabric as an unlined curtain. Refer to the introduction for advice on possible curtain headings.

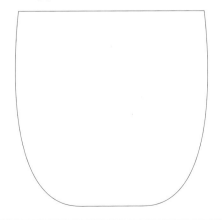

Ribbon Tie Curtain

These offcuts of patterned ribbons make pretty ties for the top of either a lined or an unlined curtain.

MATERIALS

curtain fabric

lining fabric (optional)

scissors

tape measure

ribbons

iron and ironing board

thread

needle

sewing machine

Hints

The ribbons should be placed approximately 15cm/6in apart along the top edge of the curtain. For a fuller ribbon edging, use wider ribbon and stitch the ties closer together.

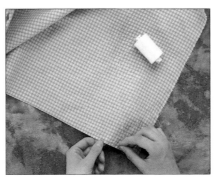

1 Select your curtain fabric, measure your window and for a lined curtain follow the instructions in the introduction. For an unlined curtain, make double 12mm/$\frac{1}{2}$in turnings for the sides (allow 2.5cm/1in on each side of the fabric for this) and a double 5cm/2in turning for the bottom hem (10cm/4in fabric allowance).

2 Cut 35.5cm/14in lengths of ribbon, fold each in half and press with a cool iron. Place the fold along the top edge of the body fabric. Cut a 10cm/4in deep border from the width of body fabric and, with right sides facing, pin and then sew this over the folded ribbons.

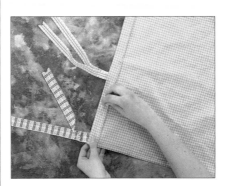

3 Fold the border over and turn under to make a double hem. Press and then stitch the hem, and turn under the raw edges at either side of the border. Sew them under to hide all raw edges. Cut the ends of the ribbons neatly and tie them onto curtain rings.

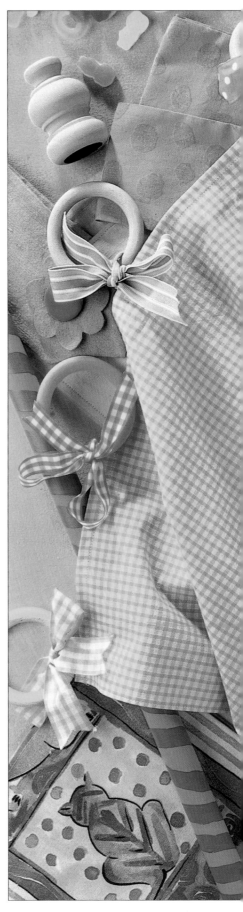

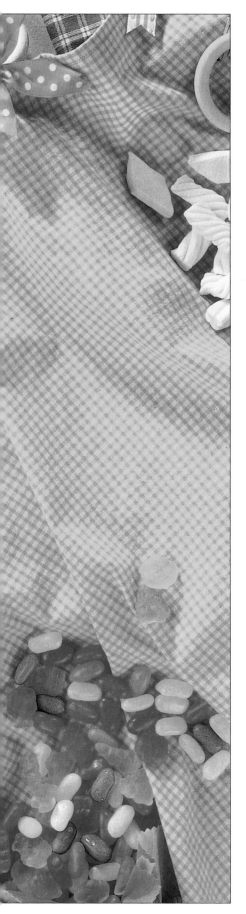

Painted Curtain Pole and Rings

Natural wood poles are ideal for painting. Use coordinating colours to match your curtains or wallpaper for a discreet look or paint bright colours for a child's room or nursery.

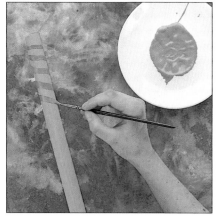

1 Paint the pole using two layers of emulsion paint and allow to dry before painting on a contrasting spiral of paint. When this is dry, seal and protect the surface using two coats of acrylic varnish.

2 Decorate the wooden rings and finials using emulsion paints. You may need a small paintbrush to paint between the curves of the end finials. Once again, protect and seal the painted surface using acrylic varnish.

MATERIALS

natural wood pole/rings

emulsion paint (various colours)

small decorator's paintbrush

acrylic varnish

Hints

Wooden poles that haven't been polished or varnished are best for painting. Use emulsion paints and seal with two layers of acrylic varnish. For polished wood you must sand down the surface prior to painting.

Scottie Dog
Appliqué

These simple Scottie dogs are
quickly made from two layers
of checked fabric and sewn to
the bottom of the curtain hem.

MATERIALS

curtain fabric

tape measure

scissors

thread

sewing machine

check ribbons

needle

tracing paper

pencil

paper

check fabric

pinking scissors

pencil

Hints

Use the fabric to make a simple headed
curtain or an eyelet blind as on pages 24-5.
Just sew under the raw edges using a double
12mm/^{1}/$_2$in hem and the bottom and top
hems should be turned under by a double
5cm/2in hem.

1   Tie short lengths of ribbon into neat little bows and sew a line of them along the top edge of the body fabric on the right side. Regularly space them at 5cm/2in intervals. Scatter and stitch more bows all over the fabric.

2   Trace the outline on this page and enlarge it on a photocopier to an appropriate size. Use the template to cut Scottie dogs from two colours of checked fabric - use pinking scissors if you have them. Stitch two dog shapes together with wrong sides facing.

3   Mark the position of each dog along the bottom edge of the hem at regular intervals with a pencil. Then stitch the dogs and bows together and sew them in place. Follow the guidelines in the introduction as to your chosen method of hanging the Scottie dog fabric at your window.

Ribbon Roll-up Blind

This blind is held on an ordinary bamboo pole using ribbons,
and the longer ribbons are used to raise and lower it.

MATERIALS

tape measure	iron and ironing board
blind fabric	sewing machine
scissors	ribbons (thin and wide)
needle and thread	bamboo pole
pins	cup hooks

Hints

Measure the window and cut the blind fabric using the guidelines in the introduction.
Leave it unlined or it will be too heavy.

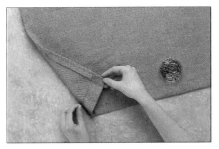

1 Sew under the sides of the fabric using a double 12mm/¹/₂in hem and turn the bottom under using a double 5cm/2in hem. Pin, stitch and then press the seams. Cut the wide ribbon into two lengths, each measuring twice the height of the window.

2 Cut 35.5cm/14in lengths of narrow ribbon, fold each in half and place the folds along the raw edge of the top of the blind, right side up, at regular intervals. Fold the wider ribbons in half and also place the folds over the raw edge. Cut a 7.5cm/3in deep border from the width of body fabric and pin this over the ribbons so that the right sides of the fabric are facing.

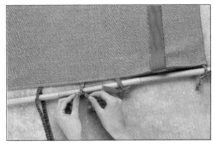

3 Stitch the border onto the body fabric along the top edge, making a seam allowance of 12mm/¹/₂in. Turn the narrow border over, press and fold the raw edges over into a double hem. Turn under the sides and stitch down. Use a sewing machine or tiny hand stitches.

4 Tie the blind to the bamboo pole with the short ribbons. Then attach the pole to the window frame by hanging it from two large cup hooks (you may wish to support the pole in the centre as well if the blind is very long). Roll up the blind and hold in place with the wide ribbon ties.

Heart Stencilled Border

With or without the stencil, this deeply bordered curtaining is best used on full-length curtains.

MATERIALS

tracing paper

pencil

paper

scissors

stencilling card

craft knife

border fabric

tape measure

muslin

thread

needle

stencilling brush

stencilling paint

heading tape

Hints

This bordered muslin creates an attractive curtain for any room in the home. Sew the border around all four sides of the curtain for the best results. When stitching the heading tape across the top of the curtain, align it with the bottom edge of the border. Cut the lightweight muslin to size only after studying my recommendations in the introduction.

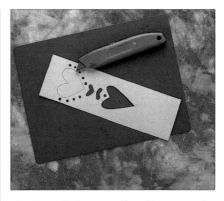

1 Trace the heart motif on this page and use a photocopier to enlarge it to an appropriate size. Transfer the image onto stencilling card and cut out the shapes between the outlines using a sharp craft knife. The width of the stencilling card should be the same width as the cotton border.

2 Cut 20cm/8in strips from the cotton fabric and join them together to make the edging borders. Fold 2.5cm/1in allowances down the sides of the strips and then fold each piece in half down its length. Sandwich the muslin between the border. To make neat mitred corners, fold the border into points at each end of the top and bottom strips.

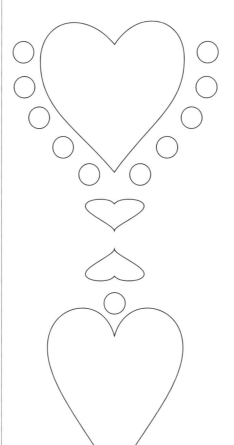

3 Fold the pointed edges over the corresponding border on the adjacent side. Hand sew the mitred edges using small invisible stitches.

4 Place the stencil on the border fabric and use a stencilling brush with a little fabric paint to paint in the design. Use a tapping motion with the brush to transfer the paint onto the cloth. Continue stencilling the design around the border. Stitch on the heading tape as described in the Hints to the left.

Cactus Stamping

Rubber stamps are a brilliant new way of decorating your own fabric and many different images are becoming available.

MATERIALS

fabric dye

plastic bowl

rubber gloves

muslin

tape measure

iron and ironing board

thread

needle

rubber stamp

fabric dye pad

ruler (optional)

tailor's chalk (optional)

Hints

If you can't find the shade of fabric that you like, dye your own inexpensive white muslin. A cold water dye is quick, easy and successful if you follow the dying instructions carefully. The patterns can then be stamped onto the fabric as rand omly as you see here or in a regular pattern. If you go for the latter, you need to mark a grid over the fabric using a ruler and tailor's chalk, printing the motif in a regular position.

1 Study the dying instructions on the back of the packet or tin and then mix it up in a plastic container using rubber gloves to prevent the dye staining your hands. Place the unfolded fabric, slightly dampened, into the dye and swish it around in the solution to dye evenly.

2 Remove the dyed fabric after the recommended time and dry it. Press the cloth and turn under the raw edges according to your curtaining option (see the introduction for ideas). Press the rubber stamp into the fabric dye pad and transfer the pattern on to the fabric.

Padded Numbers Curtain

These softly padded numbers can be attached and detached using pieces of touch-and-close fastening stitched at the back of each number and directly onto the curtain fabric. Use your existing curtains or follow the guidelines in the introduction for sewing new ones.

MATERIALS

pencil

paper

ruler

scissors

fabric pieces

pinking scissors (optional)

touch-and-close fastener

needle

thread

chopstick

stuffing

Hints

To make the numbers, draw big numbers on paper and add a border of at least 5cm/2in around each one which will give the numbers a good depth when padded. Cut the templates from the paper and use them to cut out fabric. You will need two fabric pieces for each number.

1 Use your templates (see Hints, opposite) to cut the fabric numbers. To prevent the fabric from fraying, use pinking scissors if you have them. Alternatively, use felt or another non-fraying fabric. Stitch one side of touch-and-close fastener to the back of a number and the other side to the curtains.

2 Sew each number pair together with the wrong sides facing. Keep the stitching line as close to the edge as possible and leave a small gap for stuffing. Pack the stuffing in quite tightly using a chopstick or knitting needle to push the stuffing around the curves. Sew the gap closed and stick the numbers to the curtain.

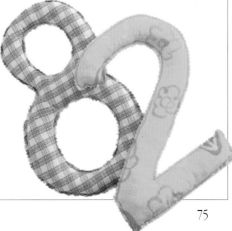

Frosted Glass Effect

Small bathroom windows are perfect for this 'trick' version of frosted glass.

MATERIALS

self-adhesive plastic

scissors

pencil

oil paint

polyurethane varnish

saucer

stencilling brush

Hints

Dab off the excess paint onto a piece of scrap paper so that you are stencilling with only a small amount of paint. Any drips are therefore kept to a minimum - essential on a vertical surface.

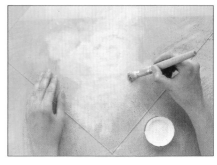

1 Cut out a variety of twists and curls from a sheet of self- adhesive plastic: draw your own or use the outlines on this page as a guide. Peel off the backing paper and place the curls on the glass.

2 Mix together equal quantities of white oil paint and polyurethane varnish; a tablespoon of each should be sufficient for a small window. Use a stencilling brush to apply the paint to the glass, tapping the brush against the surface.

3 Leave the painted surface to dry completely before removing the plastic curls and revealing the design underneath. You may need to lift up the corner of each motif with a craft knife or a pair of scissors.

Stained Glass Effect

The glorious transparent colours
of stained glass are easy to
achieve with these glass paints.

MATERIALS

self-adhesive plastic (optional)

chinagraph pencil

relief outliner

glass paints

ruler

paintbrushes

Hints

Paint the colours on the surface of the glass
when it is flat; otherwise they will run. If you
are replacing old glass, work on the new
piece before setting it into the frame. Or
paint the design on a piece of self-adhesive
plastic and stick this on the window.

1 Measure the window to determine the size of your design. For this simple ladder design, lightly draw the vertical and horizontal lines on the glass or plastic using a chinagraph pencil and a ruler, or draw freehand if you prefer a slightly wobbly line. Use the nozzle on the relief paste to fill in the lines.

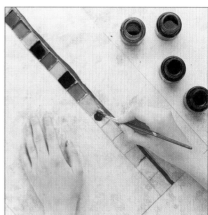

2 Fill in the areas between the relief paste with the coloured paints. Use enough paint on the paintbrush to almost flood the space and the runny paint will then fill in the shape quite naturally. Allow the paints to dry thoroughly. For the plastic stained glass, peel off the backing paper and stick in place. Remember that whatever design you choose to paint, it will be seen in reverse from the outside.

Colour-washed Blinds

Colour-washed blinds are replacing plain ones in many of the design and decorating shops, so here's a quick way of creating that up-to-the-minute look without spending a fortune.

MATERIALS

oil-based paint

turpentine

paint bucket

wooden Venetian-type blind

soft cloth

paintbrush

Hints

Open the blind to its maximum drop to paint it, and place it on several layers of newspaper to protect your work surface. Paint one side of the blind first and leave it to dry before turning the blind over to work on the other side.

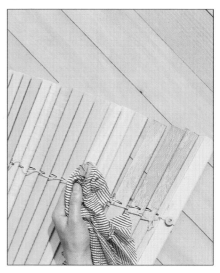

1 Mix four parts of paint to one part of turpentine in the paint bucket. For my blind I wanted quite an opaque paint, allowing only a hint of the wood colour to show through. If your blind is quite battered, this is probably your best option, but if you want a lighter look, simply add more turpentine.

2 Spread the blind in front of you so that the slats do not touch each other. Dip the soft cloth into the prepared paint. Rub the paint onto the surface of each slat as if you were cleaning it. Do not worry if the paint seeps into the cords as these look better colour-matched.

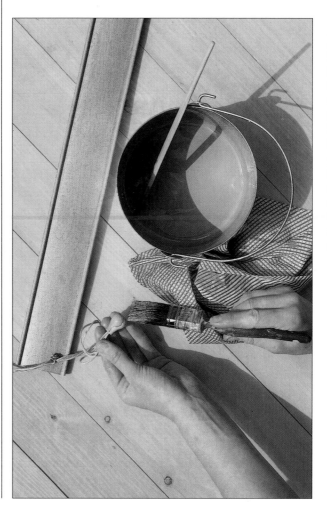

3 Use the same technique to paint the top covering strip (if your blind has one), and colour match any other parts of the blind such as the acorn cord holder on this one. On these small pieces, you may find it easier to brush on the paint and then wipe off the excess with a cloth. Use a very thin version of the paint to colour-match all the cords.

Kitchen Café Curtain

Look out for odd napkins in secondhand shops or sales. Rummaging in dusty cardboard boxes often unearths glorious finds such as these checked ones.

MATERIALS

napkins

sewing machine

thread

scissors

brass eyelets

hammer

curtain wire

curtain rings and hooks

Hints

Use napkins that are equal in size or cut larger ones to the same shape as smaller ones. You will need enough napkins to cover the width of your window plus an overlap of 15cm/6in.

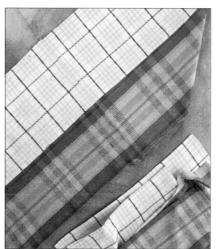

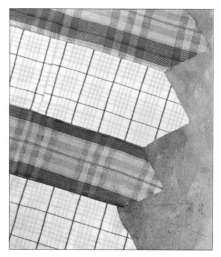

1 Cut the napkins in half lengthwise, and zigzag stitch the cut edges to prevent fraying. Fold the top left and right edges into the centre of each piece and press. Unfold them and cut along the creases to form points. Sew the long edges together and press the seams flat at the back.

2 Turn under the smallest edge possible along the edges of the points. Fold under the excess fabric at the top of the points, press, and then stitch the turnings. If the hem is uneven because the napkins weren't exactly the same size, trim the hem and stitch carefully.

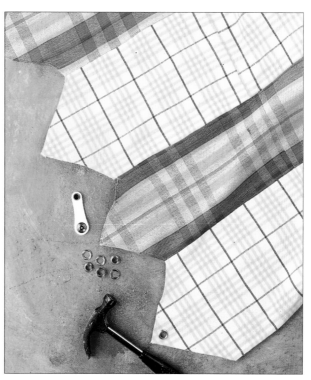

3 Using the special tool supplied with the eyelet kit, secure a brass eyelet into the top of each point. Position the curtain at the window and mark the height of the eyelet. Screw the hooks into the frame at this point and thread curtain wire through the eyelets. Stretch the curtain in place.

Tea Towel Blind

Coloured tea towels make brilliant
coverings for windows. Stitch
together as many as it takes to
cover the window.

MATERIALS

wooden batten (5 x 2.5cm/2 x 1in)

touch-and-close fastener

fabric glue

screw eyes

tape measure

tea towels

thread

scissors

casing fabric

dowelling rods

saw

curtain rings

blind cord

brass rings

acorn

cleat

Hints

To hang the blind at a window, screw a
wooden batten onto the frame. Glue one
side of a strip of touch-and-close fastener
to this. Fix screw eyes to the bottom edge
of the batten to correspond with the rings
on the blind.

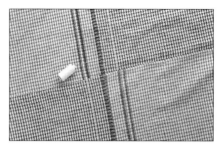

1 Measure the width and drop required to cover the window and stitch the towels together to match these measurements. If you need to piece the towels, sew a double hem at the raw edges to prevent fraying.

2 In contrasting fabric, cut strips that are 9cm/3 ¹/₂in deep and the same width as the blind plus 2.5cm/1in for the end hems. These will be the casings for the dowelling rods and the size of the window will determine how many you will need. Leave about 30cm/12in between each casing. Lay the blind flat and leaving a distance of approximately 5cm/2in from the bottom and 23cm/9in from the top, measure the position of the casings. Pin and then stitch the casings to the blind keeping the seams horizontal. Saw the dowelling to the right length and slide into the casings.

3 Sew the other half of the touch-and-close fastener to the top of the blind. Then sew the curtain rings to the bottom edge of each casing at intervals of 50cm/20in and 5cm/2in in from each edge. Thread the cord through the rings (including the batten), taking the cords to one side of the blind. Attach the blind to the batten and finally attach an acorn and cleat to hold the cords.

CHAPTER 4

Accessorizing

In this chapter there are projects for pelmets and curtain poles as well as step-by-step instructions for making your own mosaic window box and a novel approach for using ordinary mop heads as finials. Accessories can be the focal point of the window area. The decorated tin star pelmet certainly makes an impression at any window and the oversized mother-of-pearl button holdback gives a beautiful understated look when used to hold ordinary linen curtains. If you are decorating on a budget, follow the instructions for the music manuscript curtain pole. I show you how to create this elegant pole with just a length of dowelling and adapted wooden balls as finials. Decoration is even simpler with torn pieces of manuscript stuck directly around the pole. Detailed instructions make these projects not only inspiring but easy to make; and the variety of different paint techniques and fabrics are all carefully outlined to show you exactly how to recreate each project in your own home.

Manuscript Curtain Pole

A length of thick dowelling and decorator's wooden balls are easily assembled to make an inexpensive curtain pole.

MATERIALS

music manuscript	teabags
dowelling	cotton cloth
tape measure	acrylic varnish
saw	paintbrush
PVA adhesive	curtain pole rings
wooden decorator's balls	

Hints

Use torn strips of music manuscript pasted onto the pole for a unique decoration. The manuscript is painted with a solution of cold tea before it is varnished to simulate an antique finish.

1 Cut a length of dowelling to the size of your window; remember to include the length of the wooden balls at the ends. Tear small strips from the manuscript and paste them onto the wooden balls and around the dowelling pole using PVA adhesive.

2 Pour hot water onto two teabags and allow the tea to infuse and cool. Dip a small piece of cotton cloth into the tea and wipe this all over the paper manuscript. You will be able to see the colour change immediately, although it will dry slightly darker.

3 Once the tea has dried, varnish the poles and the balls. Use acrylic varnish for the quickest results. So that the varnish does not stick to anything, leave the balls to dry on a plastic surface and keep the pole propped up.

4 Slide the curtain rings onto the pole and glue on the wooden balls. Use wood adhesive applied to both surfaces for a strong setting. Hold the balls firmly against the pole for a few moments and allow the glue to set a little before releasing.

Acetate Window Decoration

Children's bedroom windows - or kitchen windows - can be made to look more cheerful with these simple acetate stickers. Use waterproof pens or ink to colour in your design and simply stick them on the glass.

MATERIALS

self-adhesive plastic

scissors

chinagraph pencil

waterproof markers/inks

paintbrushes

Hints

Waterproof markers will glide on the plastic surface easily, but coloured inks will need a second coat for a more solid colour.

1 Cut a piece of self-adhesive plastic approximately to the size of the required design. Using a chinagraph pencil lightly draw in the design's details, or use the ink directly on the surface. Paint in the separate colours. Coloured ink may resist slightly, so paint on a second coat once the first is dry.

2 Use a black marker pen or black ink to draw an outline around the coloured design. You will need to use a fine artist's paintbrush if you are using fluid ink. Add vein detailing on the leaves. Leave to dry.

3 Cut the design from the sheet using a sharp pair of scissors. Follow the outline quite carefully, but allow an extra thickness of plastic around the narrow parts of the design to make application easier. Peel away the backing paper and stick the plastic to the window.

Pelmet Swag

Patterned headscarves form
the basis of this swagged
pelmet. Floral, paisley or
striped, whatever the pattern,
almost any scarf would
look good draped
in this way.

MATERIALS

old headscarves
scissors
tape measure
thread
sewing machine
iron and ironing board
clip on curtain rings

Hints

Drape this pelmet swag around
a curtain pole to disguise an
uninteresting curtain heading
or to make a feature around
a pretty window.

1 Cut the scarves into triangles. Two of the sides should measure 28cm/11in and the third (the base) approximately 23cm/9in. Place two triangles together, right sides facing, and stitch down the two longer sides. Turn right sides out and press.

2 Make a long border that is 15cm/6in wide from strips of scarves sewn together. Halve the strip with wrong sides facing, fold the sides in to meet the centre line and press flat. Insert the base of each triangle inside the border strip, sew together and hang from pole using clip on curtain rings.

Punched Pelmet

This pelmet looks particularly attractive when positioned above a thin voile curtain so that the light diffuses through the fine material and its tiny pinprick holes.

MATERIALS

fusible buckram

scissors

pelmet fabric

tape measure

iron and ironing board

tracing paper

pencil

paper

darning needle

hammer

nail

staple gun

ribbon

fabric glue

Hints

In a small window where there is no need for curtains, use this punched pelmet on a reduced scale to add a decorative detail. Staple or tack the pelmet onto a pelmet board and cover the line of staples with a length of ribbon.

1 Cut the fusible buckram to the exact size required for your window. Cut plain cotton fabric to this size plus 2.5cm/1in all around for turning. Fuse the buckram onto the cotton with a hot iron, turning under the allowances. Trace the outline on this page and enlarge it on a photocopier to an appropriate size. Cut a template from the outline and use it to draw the motif along the bottom of the buckram pelmet. Cut out the design with scissors.

2 Copy the dots from the outline on this page onto the template and then position the template over the detailed edge. Push a darning needle through the dots as a guide for the punched holes. Then place the detailed edge against a piece of wood and use a hammer and nail to punch out the holes. Staple the pelmet to a board above the window frame and disguise the staples by gluing a ribbon over them.

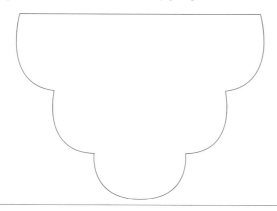

Buttoned Holdbacks

These oversized buttons are covered with lots and lots of tiny
mother-of-pearl buttons stitched on padded bases.

MATERIALS

plywood or MDF	fabric
saucer	scissors
pencil	thread
fret saw	needle
dowelling	wadding
tape measure	mother-of-pearl buttons
wood glue	double-ended screws

Hints

These holdbacks are traditionally round, but you could cut almost any shape
you wish - diamonds would look good, as would squares or hexagons.

1 Cut the holdbacks from a piece of plywood or MDF. Draw the outlines around a saucer and then cut them out with a fret saw. For each holdback, cut a length of thick dowelling approximately 15cm/6in and use wood glue to stick the pieces of dowelling to the underside of the circles.

2 For each holdback, cut a disc of fabric using the MDF base as a guide, and allowing 2.5cm/1in all around for turning. Sew a running stitch around the outside of the fabric circle approximately 12mm/^{1}/$_2$in from the edge.

3 Cut a circle of wadding to the same size as the MDF holdback. Hold the wadding and the circle of fabric together and sew on the mother-of-pearl buttons, starting from the centre and working outwards. Sew the buttons through the thick wadding.

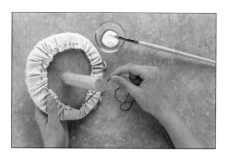

4 Pull the running stitch threads and slip the circular holdback inside. Spread glue along the inside edge and then pull up the threads still further. Sew the threads to secure and then attach the holdbacks to the wall with double-ended screws.

Gilded Shell Pole

Use either the flat part or the curved top of these pretty shells.

MATERIALS

dowelling	wood glue
saw	PVA adhesive
shells	Dutch metal leaf (or gold paint)
yellow emulsion paint	acrylic varnish
paintbrush	pole rings
drawer handles	bonding glue

Hints

If it is difficult to obtain small quantities of Dutch metal leaf, use gold paint. But make sure it is good quality - you can usually tell by the price, and cheaper paints are often rather dull.

1 Cut a length of dowelling to the size of the required pole; remember to exclude the finial ends. Paint this and the shells with a coat of pale yellow emulsion paint. You will also need to paint two small drawer handles to attach to the ends of the pole.

2 Use strong wood glue to secure the drawer handles to the ends of the dowelling pole. Hold the two pieces together for a little while to make sure they are firmly stuck together. Release and allow to dry completely.

3 Brush a thin layer of PVA adhesive over the pole (but not the drawer handles) and the front of the shells. When it is almost dry - the glue should be tacky - press the metal leaf over the surface and it should adhere easily. Remove the backing paper and rub away the excess foil. Paint on a coat of acrylic varnish and leave to dry.

4 If you are using rings, slide them onto the pole and then use a strong bonding glue to attach the shells onto the ends. If the shells are flat, bonding is slightly easier. Curved shells may need propping forward with a piece of cork or wood so that they lie straight.

Tin Star Pelmet

The recycling trend is upon us! These metal stars are formed from empty tubes of tomato paste: let's hope the manufacturers don't start to use plastic.

MATERIALS

plywood or MDF (thinnest width)

tape measure

saw

tracing paper

pencil

paper

scissors

fret saw

emulsion paint (2 colours)

paintbrushes

wax polish

cloth

sandpaper (coarse-grade)

empty tomato paste tubes

blunt scissors

old ballpoint pen

bonding glue

right-angled brackets

screws (2 sizes)

Hints

Attach this pelmet to the wall using angled brackets. If the corners need boxing in, cut two smaller pieces from MDF or plywood and attach them to the front of the pelmet at right angles with strong wood glue, to form three sides of a rectangle.

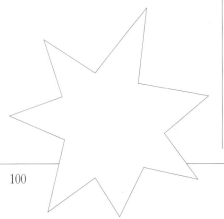

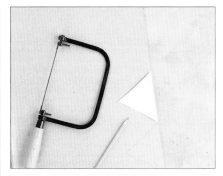

1 Carefully cut a sheet of plywood or MDF to the size of the finished pelmet. Then make a suitably-sized equilateral triangle and use this as a template to draw a serated edge along the bottom of the pelmet. Cut out the detailed edge using a fret saw.

2 Paint the front of the pelmet board with your chosen base colour and leave it to dry. Then wipe a thin layer of wax polish unevenly over the surface of the base coat. This will form a resist layer between the undercoat and top coat of paint and makes distressing the colour easier.

3 Paint on the top colour and allow the paint to dry completely. Distress the paint by rubbing the surface with a coarse-grade sandpaper. The paint should distress easily because of the wax resist layer underneath.

4 Cut the top and bottom off the tomato paste tube with a pair of old scissors. Cut down the length of the tube, open it out and wash with warm soapy water. Trace the template on this page and enlarge it on a photocopier to an appropriate size. Draw this star onto the metal sheet.

Starry Curtain

The same tin stars that adorn the pelmet are used to add a decorative flourish to a plain curtain.

MATERIALS

curtain fabric

template (as opposite)

empty tomato paste tubes

blunt scissors

old ballpoint pen

hammer

nail

needle

thread

Hints

Choose a fabric that is thicker than fine voile as the reverse side of the stars still remain printed with the tomato paste logo.

5   Cut the metal stars using a blunt pair of scissors. Turn the stars over and use the depressed end of a old ballpoint pen to score the patterns onto the metal stars. The metal is quite soft so you should not need to use too much pressure for the marks to show up. Use strong bonding glue to attach the metal stars to the pelmet board and hang the pelmet with right- angled brackets.

1   Cut out the stars and decorate the surface of the tin following steps 4 and 5 carefully as outlined in the Tin Star Pelmet project opposite. Use a hammer and nail to punch a hole through the top of one point on each star.

2   Sew the tin stars onto the curtain. Stitch the stars at random, trying not to form a regular pattern. As there is not a vast amount of sewing involved, you may be able to sew the stars onto the curtain without having to remove it first.

Crackled Shell Pelmet with Shells

This pelmet would be perfectly suited to a bathroom, or in a child's room where the shells can capture the children's attention.

MATERIALS

plywood or MDF

tape measure

saw

fret saw

emulsion paint (2 colours)

paintbrushes

crackle varnish

shells

sandpaper (coarse-grade)

bonding glue

right-angled brackets

screws

Hints

Cut out a wavy edge from a sheet of plywood. Follow the instructions outlined for the Tin Star Pelmet on the previous page.

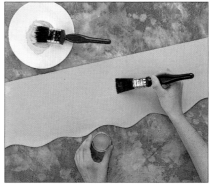

1 Paint the pelmet with two coats of a medium blue emulsion paint. Leave it to dry thoroughly and then apply a thin layer of crackle varnish. Paint the varnish in one direction only.

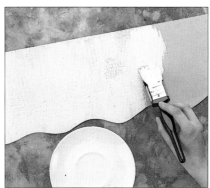

2 Paint a layer of cream emulsion paint over the dry crackle varnish. Load the paintbrush with paint and work quickly; you will see the cracks start forming almost as soon as the emulsion paint goes on. Leave to dry.

3 To make bonding easier, rub the base of each shell with a coarse-grade sandpaper to scratch the surface underneath. Use a strong bonding glue to glue the shells along the edge of the pelmet. Attach the pelmet as for the Tin Star Pelmet on the previous page.

Cactus Appliqué Pelmet

These cacti are stunning shapes to work with but as their outlines are so basic they are delightfully simple to stitch.

MATERIALS

tape measure

fusible buckram

scissors

pelmet fabric

iron and ironing board

tracing paper

pencil

paper

fabric scraps

tailor's chalk

fabric glue

fabric trimmings

embroidery thread

needle

glue/staple gun

ribbon (optional)

Hints

Use odd assortments of fabric scraps for the appliqué as it looks infinitely better when the cacti are composed of different patterns and textures. A piece of towelling makes one of my cacti look impressive.

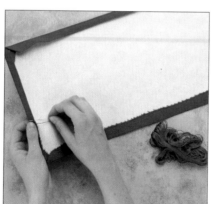

1 Measure the window area and use a strong pair of scissors to cut a piece of fusible buckram to the size of the finished pelmet. Cut a piece of coloured fabric to this size plus 2.5cm/1in all around for turnings. Use a hot iron to fuse the buckram to the cotton.

2 Trace the outlines on this page and enlarge them on a photocopier to an appropriate size. Use these as templates for the cacti and their pots. Cut the appliqué pieces from different fabrics. As the pelmet isn't intended to be washed you can mix all sorts of different cloths.

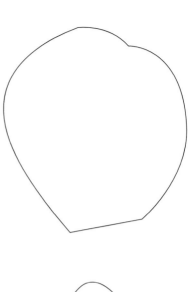

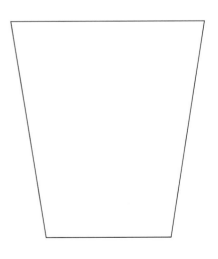

3 Mark the positions of the cacti pots on the pelmet using a piece of tailor's chalk; the pots should be approximately 15cm/6in apart. Use fabric glue to attach the cacti to the face of the fabric pelmet. Small pieces of fabric trimmings can be used across the top of the pots.

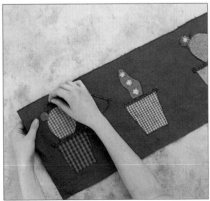

4 Use embroidery thread to work the overstitches, as above. Use different colours of thread and different lengths of stitches to create the whimsical characters of each cactus. Glue or staple the pelmet to the pelmet board. If stapling, glue a length of ribbon over them.

Fruity Découpage Pelmet

This pretty scalloped edge flatters any window and could be used to disguise an unattractive curtain head or, positioned above the window frame, to make a smaller window appear larger.

MATERIALS

plywood or MDF

tape measure

saw

source material

watercolour paints

paintbrush

paper glue

glue brush

acrylic varnish

right-angled brackets

screws

Hints

Cut almost any découpage motif from magazines, catalogues or source books. In a kitchen, these fruity images look particularly good, but you could use vegetables, flowers or butterflies - whatever attracts your eye.

1 Follow step 1 outlined in the Tin Star Pelmet on page 100 for directions on cutting the pelmet board, making scallops rather than points. If you need to make corner returns for the sides make them also as described in the Tin Star Pelmet Hints. Paint the surface with the base colour.

2 Cut out the images from their source book. Use a photocopier if you need to reproduce the same image several times and tint the images with watercolour paints. A simple wash should be all that is required.

3 Decide on the arrangement of the images on the pelmet and then glue them in place with strong paper glue. When the glue is thoroughly dry, protect the pelmet board with two coats of acrylic varnish. Leave to dry and then attach the board to the angled brackets as described in the introduction.

Mop Head
Curtain Pole

Unusual and certainly different,
these brightly coloured mop heads
provide brilliant finials for a
less-than-interesting window.

MATERIALS

cold water dye

large plastic container

rubber gloves

2 new mop heads

dowelling

fabric pieces

pinking scissors

ribbon

pole rings

cup hooks or pole brackets

Hints

Use the mop handle as the curtain pole
if it is long enough; otherwise, buy a length
of dowelling. Paint the pole and curtain
rings with emulsion paint to match the
dyed mop heads.

1 Use a cold water dye to colour the new mop heads. Wearing rubber gloves, mix the solution in a large plastic container and swish the heads around in the dye until they have absorbed the colour. Squeeze out the excess dye and leave to dry.

2 Cut two 38cm/15in-diameter circles from different coloured fabrics using pinking scissors. Snip a hole in the centre of one circle and slide it over a mop. Cover the end with the other circle and push into the finial. Slide on the pole rings.

3 Repaet step 2 for the other end of the pole. Then use a coordinating ribbon to tie a bow around the top of each circle of fabric to neaten. Secure the pole to the window frame using cup hooks that the pole simply drops into, or use pole brackets.

Mosaic Window Box

This ceramic mosaic is constructed from broken pieces of china. Scour secondhand shops and car boot sales for odd cups, saucers and plates.

MATERIALS

terracotta planter	emulsion paint
china	grout/adhesive
newspaper/plastic bags	rubber gloves (optional)
hammer	cloth
old spoon and knife	

Hints

Place the china pieces in a plastic bag or between several sheets of newspaper, then tap sharply with a hammer. Remove the larger pieces and throw away the smaller ones.

1 Stir approximately two tablespoons of coloured emulsion paint into a quantity of tile adhesive/grout. Use an old spoon to mix the paste together. Mix small quantities at first, making more as you need it.

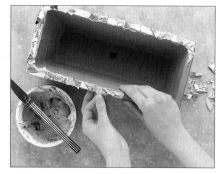

2 Use an old kitchen knife to spread a generous layer of tile adhesive/grout onto the rim of the planter. Select pieces of ceramic and push these firmly into the paste. Any sharp pieces that jut out can be tapped off later when the mosaic is set.

3 Working slowly down the sides of the planter. Apply the paste and press in the ceramic pieces, then apply more paste and continue until the planter is covered. Try to place straight edges of ceramic against the sides of the planter.

4 Leave the grout to stand for about an hour before using it to fill in the gaps between the ceramic pieces. Use your finger to do this (wear an old rubber glove if your skin is sensitive). Wipe excess grout from the surface with a damp cloth.

ACKNOWLEDGMENTS

The publishers would like to thank the following companies and people for providing the merchandise used in our photographs:

Anchor Threads, Coats Patons Crafts, Darlington, DL1 1YQ
Tel: 0325 381010

Dylon International   Tel: 081 663 4801

Fun Stamps Ltd, 144 Neilston Road, Paisley PA2 6QJ
Tel: 041 884 6441   Fax: 041 884 7819

General Trading Company, 144 Sloane Square, London SW1X

Gore Booker, 44 Bedford Street, Covent Garden, London WC2H

The Museum Store, 37 The Market, The Piazza, Covent Garden,
London WC2H

Nice Irma's, 46 Goodge Street, London W1

Mildred Pearce, 33 Earlham Street, Covent Garden,
London WC2H

Purves and Purves, 80-81 Tottenham Court Road, London W1

GLOSSARY

US readers may not be familiar with the following terms:

UK	US
blind	window shade
centre	center
chinagraph	china marker pen
colour(s) (ed)	color
dinner jacket	tuxedo
emulsion paint	latex paint
favourite	favorite
fibre	fiber
forefinger	index finger
fretsaw	scroll saw
frilled	ruffled
lengthways	lengthwise
MDF	particle board
mitre(d) (s)	miter
muslin	cheesecloth
music manuscript	sheet music
neaten	finish (seams, etc)
PVA glue	white craft glue
pelmet	valance
pinking scissors	pinking shears
tea towel	dish towel
turnings	seam allowance or hem
wadding	batting